UNDERESTIMATE ME.
That'll be fun!

FURIOSA

Underestimate me. That'll be fun!
Copyright © 2021 by Furiosa

All rights reserved. No part of this publication may be reproduced, distributed, or transmitted in any form or by any means, including photocopying, recording, or other electronic or mechanical methods, without the prior written permission of the author, except in the case of brief quotations embodied in critical reviews and certain other non-commercial uses permitted by copyright law.

Tellwell Talent
www.tellwell.ca

ISBN
978-0-2288-5523-1 (Hardcover)
978-0-2288-5522-4 (Paperback)
978-0-2288-5524-8 (eBook)

CONTENTS

Preface v

1. I am a nice girl. I carry an axe. 1
2. It's your life. Choose your own adventure. 2
3. "Eminence Front" 5
4. One life. Just one. 10
5. Franken-friends 12
6. The Doll 17
7. Going along to get along and staying stuck 19
8. Who the Hell are you? 21
9. Grow up? Never! 23
10. Living and Existing 24
11. Hell's magnet and the devil 25
12. She Devils 27
13. Food for the soul 31
14. Stargazing 33
15. Into the Depths 36
16. Dorian Gray 37
17. Superpowers 39
18. Mess is a matter of perspective 40
19. Inner Voice 41
20. Power of Silence 42
21. Planet Furiosa 44
22. Beautiful noise 45
23. Let It Go 46
24. Be brave 47
25. Ghosting and mosting 49

26. Deal with it, whatever it is..54
27. Take a Leap..55
28. Living vs Existing..56
29. Social media—the human rock tumbler..........................57
30. Where the hell are you?..61
31. Spilled milk is one of the four main food groups.............63
32. Nobody's business but your own......................................65
33. Crazy women and men as victims....................................67
34. The filter..69
35. Keeping it real...70
36. "Music is my aeroplane…"..72
37. Love..73
38. Twin Flames..77
39. Revenge..79
40. Leave your mark..80
41. Gratitude—grab some...81
42. Lab Rat..83
43. Say it!...86
44. Failure—A Blessing..88

PREFACE

I am a curious human who prefers to live rather than just exist. It's okay to get lost on the way to making your place in the world. Know that the pain you must endure to get there, the struggle and upheaval, is less intense and suffocating than staying paralyzed in fear and regret, stuck where your heart, soul, and mind know damned well you don't belong.

Abandon Groupthink All Who Enter Here

1

I am a nice girl. I carry an axe.

It has a red blade that matches the soles of my Louboutins. Why do I carry an axe? Sometimes people mistake my friendly smile and generosity of spirit for weakness and are rude, so I have to chop them into pieces. Mine is, of course, a verbal axe, and I am not afraid to use it. I can be your dearest, most loyal friend, or I can be your worst enemy. The great thing is you get to choose which one I will be.

It's your life. Choose your own adventure.

> "Don't follow me, I will get you lost. Don't lead because I will get bored and wander off. Just walk beside me and help me cause trouble."
>
> —Unknown Author

I write this book for me, though I know some people will relate to some parts of it. It's about realizing that you've been right all along—you are strange, and you are not 'normal', and that's okay. The thing that you must realize is that we are all unique, so, contrary to what society tells you, being strange and not normal, unless you're a serial killer or other obvious degenerate, is a good thing. Just forget about society and stop trying to fit in. That will only squash your potential and kill your soul, and it will be a slow, painful death.

I've come to learn many valuable things through my own experiences observing and interacting with humans and some entities that were questionably human, both on the internet and in so-called real life. These interactions affected me and enabled me to be who I really am, and they helped me get closer to peace.

Sounds cliché and hoary but it's the truth, and it's a fabulous thing when that light goes on. If you can read this book and find one little nugget that helps you realize that the only person you should allow to judge you and the only person you should give your power to is you, or even if reading it just makes you snigger, chortle, or chuckle, even at my expense, I would be ecstatic. However, I don't write this as a how-to book or a 'you should do this and then you will be that' preachy thing. I've read a ton of self-help books and what the authors did to get where they say they are is great for them. The books were usually entertaining and a good study of human behaviour, which I love, but I needed something different. One size does not fit all when you're trying to get comfortable in your own skin. Sigh... I so wanted to avoid using that well-worn but very misunderstood expression because I have said I was comfortable in my own skin when I was not. You don't know what it means until you truly are comfortable in your own skin and can declare it with certitude and scream it from a mountain. You don't know what you don't know until you really know it and then you realize how little you still know. Know what I mean? I think even Lee Michaels knows what I mean.

Previously, when I claimed to be comfortable in my own skin, I actually had lingering doubts and lacked confidence in some areas, but I thought I was as close to it as I was ever going to get. You must define 'it'. Don't judge yourself by someone else's standards, especially not by society's standards. Now? I am totally happy with me just as I am, and some would say annoyingly so. That said, I am and always will be working on myself. I am a human being under construction and in need of many repairs and upgrades. How I got here may not work for you, and as I said, you can't follow me because I will get you lost. Getting lost is not necessarily a bad thing but it's better once you are comfortable with who you are. I was lost in Valparaiso, Chile, once but knew I had at least six more hours of sunlight, so I took the nearest funicular up to a café overlooking the ocean and ordered a piece of mango raspberry cheesecake and a fresh cup of espresso. Real coffee is hard to find in Chile as most restaurants offer Nescafe instant or coca leaves for making tea. Take the coca leaves! They are on most breakfast buffets as you get further up in the Andes and are good for combatting altitude sickness and you won't miss coffee. Unfortunately, they won't let you bring the whole leaves back to the USA or Canada unless they've been stomped on or decocainized, but I digress. After enjoying the view for a long while, I slowly made my way back to home base with no problem using the water and various building landmarks as my guide.

3

"Eminence Front"

"Eminence Front" is a great song by The Who, and they are right: "it is a put on." Your game face or whatever you want to call it is a necessary thing but one you should not use often as it can be exhausting being fake when you really don't need to. Your own front is much more powerful, trust me. To crack open your eminence front and pack it away for emergencies, you have to be honest with yourself and others, and that leaves you open to attacks. The attacks and how you deal with them make you what you are. That's the whole point of my method, and for the most part I bucked the of idea pretending to be something or someone other than what I am.

Certainly, I took gobs of wisdom from here and there and tried applying them to my life—think square peg, round hole. I came to reject the whole idea that I need to be what everyone else said I should be. The one thing I knew for sure was that conformity was not an option. I also learned that while I had no control over some things that happen to me, I do have control over how I react to those things.

What I needed to be was me. Since I am better and always get done what I have to do when backed into a corner, I threw myself into the belly of the beast, facing me head on and changing myself for the better. Fear of the unknown usually kept me from doing things that had to be done, and I usually just sat there sweating with a twisted knot in my stomach waiting to be hit with a shit storm of deadlines and demands for action. This time I ran up to meet the shit storm and I killed it. I was Queen of Confrontation. You have to throw yourself into situations that scare you to conquer your fears. What doesn't kill ya makes ya stronger and all that rot. There's a saying and a song that go: "If you're going through Hell, keep going." Know that when you're in the middle of Hell there is a better place once you break on through the wall at the end, and you will get there if you don't give up. You do not fail until you stop trying. Think about that!

Confronting the shit storm as it approaches allows you to do it on your terms. It's okay to say out loud that you have no idea if what you are about to do is right but you're gonna do it anyway. I'll bet if you look back at things you didn't do because of fear of failure, you'll realize that many of those times you watched someone else do exactly what you thought should be done instead of doing the thing that scares you. Now, you probably think to yourself, *Why the hell didn't I just do it?* Depending on what that job was, no one can kill you for making a mistake, or better yet, you can ask for help. It's okay to be vulnerable. Wear your vulnerability like a frickin' diamond encrusted tiara or a Kentucky Derby chapeau.

Take what your inner voice says with a grain of salt and a shot of tequila, if necessary, but make up your own mind. Your inner voice can throw out a lot of negativity, and you have to tamp it down. It will mock you with the images of failure and humiliation. It can have you crying on street corners in the middle of the afternoon, and it can keep you up at night. Analyze the negatives it hurls at you, and you'll know most of it is absolute rubbish.

Take in what your inner voice and other people tell you, but the most important conversation you will have is the one you will have with yourself. Do not let your inner voice talk to you in a way that you wouldn't let your friends talk to you. Don't let it scare you with worse case scenarios and silly notions of what others will think.

What do you think? That is what matters. Your inner voice will give you good advice mixed in with lies you know aren't true. Do not use the lies as an excuse not to act.

Stop trying to be normal. Stop trying to fit in if it leaves you feeling uncomfortable. Lose that eminence front. Always follow your dreams, and start doing that now. Stop making excuses and procrastinating. Now is the right time. At the end of every day, you should be able to state one thing that you did that day to get you closer to your goal. If you can't, why not?

Inner Voice: You really should tone it down a bit. You are really strange... not normal, and I mean that in a bad way. You are not going to be able to handle writing a book. Is this your eminence front talking? Snicker...

Furiosa: Friendly reminder from Jake Remington: "Fate whispers to the warrior, 'You can not withstand the storm.' The warrior whispers back, 'I am the storm.'"

"I used to think I was the strangest person in the world but then I thought, there are so many people in the world, there must be someone just like me who feels bizarre and flawed in the same ways I do. I would imagine her and imagine that she must be out there thinking of me, too. Well, I hope that if you are out there you read this and know that, yes, it's true, I'm here, and I'm just as strange as you."

—Frida Kahlo

One life. Just one.

One life. Just one. Why aren't we running like we are on fire towards our wildest dreams?

—Unknown Author

It is true that if you want to know where you will be in five years, you just need to look at where your friends are right now. I knew I was stuck, and it was time to start looking at the people I associated with.

It's very queer the way your friends and others closest to you will try to talk you out of doing things that might change your world and, more importantly (to them), take you out of theirs. They don't want you going for your dreams because they have long since given up on theirs. They want you staying right where you are. They don't want you leaving the bubble and going to another bubble they cannot go to because they are afraid to follow you there. It would mean they have to take chances. They clutch their pearls and fret about what the neighbours, their friends, their family, and society might think. So, they settle for the bubble they are in. You should never settle for anything less than what you deserve. Friendly reminder: the only person you should allow to judge you and the only person you should give your power to is you.

I was surrounded by zombies who were dissatisfied with their lives but were willing to settle, even if it meant being absolutely miserable. I decided to grab some courage and be me. This time, when I met resistance from my friends, instead of caving in and going along to get along with their predictions that my dreams would bring about certain doom, abject failure, humiliation, and the end of my life as I knew it, I stood my ground.

Out of my way, zombies! This meant, of course, that I would be seeing some of my friends less and less, but as I moved forward, I was attracting kindred souls and experiencing new things. I got to the point where staying stuck was more painful and suffocating than any pain or humiliation that could come from trying to reach for the dreams my heart incessantly reminded me were my destiny.

Often friends will say to me, "I wish I could be you, taking chances, doing new things, travelling to faraway places by yourself." What they mean is they wish they could be themselves and not let opportunities pass them by. They obviously want to do the same things I do, but they choose not to. Why? They should see that I did these things and I'm still here and, I might add, I am better for it.

One of the most motivational songs, in my opinion, is "Lose Yourself" by Eminem. When an opportunity comes around, you have to grab it with both hands because it may not come around again. So go for it!

It's better to regret the things you did than the things you did not do.

Inner voice: Eminem? We're taking advice from Eminem?

Furiosa: Who is this *we* you keep talking about?

5

Franken-friends

Who the hell are these people and how did I lose me?

I will share something personal that happened to me, but I know many people have experienced similar things. I watched many of my friends, male and female, succumb to taking the easy way out and into a quick descent into conformity Hell. One day about five years ago, I looked around at my friends and coworkers and thought, *Who the fuck are these people?* In fact, I wondered who the fuck just about everyone I had contact with was. I felt like an alien that had been ejected from a spaceship and had plummeted to Earth under cover of a blast of chem trails into someone else's life. Like an amnesia victim waking up after many years, I didn't recognize anyone, not even myself. How did I lose me? I did, however, realize I had been a zombie going through the motions for too long, just like the people surrounding me. I had conformed. One difference, though, was that the people around me seemed somewhat content—except the ones on anti-depressants. Those people, God bless them, seemed zoned out and just there—not happy, not sad, just there. Their expressionless faces looked like those weird plastic jack o' lanterns with the melting facial features. These were my Franken-friends.

I didn't feel sick, but I felt more than a little off. I spoke with my family doctor about this because I couldn't accept feeling this way anymore and, of course, a busy doctor's answer is antidepressants since most people just want a pill to pop that will quickly 'fix' what ails them or mask the symptoms of what ails them instead of finding the cause. Sorry, doc! I'm not depressed. My problem is not that my body lacks human-made chemicals to alter my brain function and mood. That's what wine, Fireball, and pot are for. So, my search began. Three agonizing years of visiting anyone who would listen. A psychologist who kept telling me I had beautiful eyes, a priest who suggested I go to Brazil and work with poor children, and a psychiatrist who refused to see me again because I was normal (the latter was clearly a fucking quack because I feel insulted by being called normal when I don't feel normal).

My last resort, and the one with the best answers, was a psychic… Yeah, yeah, I know, but she was the only one who said anything that made sense, and that's how I knew it was all up to me. Obviously, I had two choices: take antidepressants and join my living crack o' lantern zombie friends in losing another decade or more of my life or keep searching for peace of mind or just peace.

I chose to keep searching and hoped the angst I felt about wasting my time and my creativity because of fear of failure or of what others might think would pass. To this day it hasn't passed completely, but I have learned to use it to push me to keep learning and experiencing life and finding my way back to me. It is a blessing—a much-needed kick in the bloomers to wake the Hell up and see the amazing and magnificent world right in front of me. I concentrate on improving myself, physically and mentally. I got rid of negative people, just chopped them right out of my life. See? That axe does come in handy. I changed my diet a little and got more exercise, and I listened to my heart and to my body when they told me what I needed. Yours are talking to you too—you have to learn to listen to them. I decided to be totally me instead of what everyone said I should be. It took a while and I swear I have more guardian angels than anyone I know because I put myself in some scary places and came out relatively unscathed. Thank you to my angels everywhere. Thank you especially to the ones placed here on Earth to watch over me, though at a distance, for your love and your support. You were always there. You were literally a 24-7 lifeline, and for that I am eternally grateful. You were my strength and my light as I crossed the Rubicon. I have some badass guardian angels.

Inner voice: What about what you put me through? This is when you stopped listening to me. I'm here to help. I know what's best for you.

Furiosa: Excuse me? The entire time you waged war on me. You told me I wasn't good enough, pretty enough, smart enough… You told me I was stupid and ungrateful and that I should just settle back into the life I had, which, considering what an idiot I am (according to you), I should have been happy to have. You were putting out the fires of my private Hell with gasoline. I guess I should thank you for dragging me to rock bottom and backing me into a corner that I had to claw my way out of.

Inner voice: You're welcome. That was my plan… cough… yes, that's it! That was my plan. Snicker…

6

The Doll

There are plenty of people who will take advantage of your willingness to be what they want you to be. I now acknowledge that these are not my friends. Now I am me, totally and unapologetically me. It's a great feeling. I see my old self in people that go along to get along, and it makes me wince. It's something you have to change for yourself. You have to get to the point where you would rather be alone and be yourself than be what someone else wants you to be just so you are with someone else. People who want your friendship and love only when they want it need to be gone. I will no longer be that always-smiling, nice to be around, pretty doll sitting on a shelf waiting to be played with only when the so-called 'friend' wants my company, yet they ignore me or are busy when I want their company.

They come take their doll off the shelf and play with it until they are bored and/or they break it, then they put the pieces of the doll back on the shelf util next time. Yeah—you people know who you are. You need to get a pet, a hooker, or just grow up and learn to treat people properly and with respect. Fuck you all in spades! But I'm not bitter... much.

Signed,

Doll no more!

Inner voice: Meh, you sound bitter.

Furiosa: I AM NOT #@!&*%$# BITTER!!

Inner voice: BITTER! PARTY OF ONE! BITTER! YOUR TABLE IS READY!

Furiosa: #@!&*%$# #@!&*%$#!!!!

Going along to get along and staying stuck

Who are you? Can you answer the question without giving your name, occupation, age, or other stats? Are you really you or are you the person other people want you to be? I was, for the most part, the latter for the first half of my life.

When I was younger, I went along with people and did things I didn't want to do, even though I was unhappy doing them, because I just wanted to be with my friends. I couldn't stand being alone. That would mean I had to listen to my inner voice aka Satan, and at that point I had no way of reasoning with it. Now if I don't want to do something, I don't do it. If I want to do something and others don't, I'll do it even if I do it alone. If I had a nickel for every time someone said to me, "You're not going to go there alone" and then I did indeed go there alone, I'd be filthy rich. It was a bumpy, nerve-wracking, and sometimes frightening start but now? Fabulous and fierce. Some say I'm arrogant and that I am (fill in the blank while I bat my eyelashes innocently, throw my head back, and laugh uproariously) but I know my flaws very well. I know I'm not perfect and I don't care, and neither should you.

I am working on the flaws that bring me grief and honing the ones that bring my enemies grief. I'm a bitch that way. I know I am broken, but beautifully so and I am flawed, but I am fabulously flawed. I have patched myself back together with stardust, ocean water, and the crazy glue of laughter, and I like what I have become. I am the result of everything that I have chosen to do and what I have allowed others to do to me. I make my own choices, as we all do, and I accept the consequences of those choices. I own them. I make my own limits, thank you very much, and then I push them. Don't bother telling me I cannot do something because I will do it if I want to. So yes, I am as arrogant as a broken and flawed person can be. I am fragile and feminine and give my heart too easily, but I am also confident, independent, and strong when I need to be. So, I learned that if my friends are trying to hold me back and telling me my plans are too big and that I should be happy where I am, I now know that I don't need new plans—I need new friends. If my friends mock my dreams because they themselves have stopped dreaming, it's time to leave those friends in their safe little bubbles.

How do you feel when you leave your friends? Do you feel encouraged and loved or discouraged and beaten down? If it's the latter, it's time to leave them behind. Your inner voice is negative enough. You don't need a pack of jealous jackals putting you down. If you are in the same spot that you were two years ago, it's time to move your ass. Seriously, every single night before you go to sleep you should be able to write down in your journal the thing or things you accomplished that day to get you closer to your goal. You should be able to write down any roadblocks that came up and what you did about them or what you will do about them to get back at it asap. Writing down your goals ensures you will work towards them.

Inner voice: That's cruel. Leave your friends? Why?

Furiosa: Because fuck them, that's why. I will only stop dreaming when I die.

8

Who the Hell are you?

An online friend asked me recently, jokingly perhaps, "Who are you?"

Without missing a beat, I typed the following:

I am Me

I am a human being under construction

I am Me

I am not normal because conformity is certain death to my soul

I am Me

Beautifully broken and fabulously flawed

I am Me

And that is my superpower

Inner voice: Woo-wee! Someone is full of themselves today.

Furiosa: And someone else is full of something, too.

Grow up? Never!

I am not 20 or 30 or… well, I'm not a kid anymore. Have you noticed that after the age of 20ish no one asks you anymore what you want to be when you grow up? No longer do the people we know indulge our dreams that involve creative occupations like dancing, painting, playing an instrument, or writing. Do we only get to dream and create until we graduate high school or college and then it's off to that conformity chain gang to break rocks five days a week for the rest of our lives? We should never stop wanting to do something new or be something else.

I have no idea what I want to be when I grow up or if I even want to grow up at all. I watched many of my friends, male and female, succumb to taking the easy way out. If you ask me what I want to be today the answer will be different than in a year from now. Grow up? No way, Jose! Noperdoodles!

Inner voice: Um, yeah, maybe you should grow up.

Furiosa: Um, yeah, maybe you should shut the fuck up!

Inner voice: Oh! That's not very mature.

Furiosa: Is too!

Inner voice: Noperdoodles!

Living and Existing

"To live is the rarest thing in the world. Most people merely exist, that is all."

—Oscar Wilde

I cry a lot for the same reason I laugh a lot. I am living and not merely existing, unlike so many people around me who are going through the motions of life and stifling their emotions and their desire to express themselves by reacting to the world around them. Tears of joy, tears of sorrow, it's all good, and I believe it is a necessary thing.

Inner Voice: Yeah! Yeah! Yeah! Living, not existing. We get it!

Furiosa: Do you?

11

Hell's magnet and the devil

I was raised Catholic, and the fear of God was only slightly less scary than the fear of the Devil, eternal Hellfire, and damnation. I was in grade 3 or 4 and I recall getting 'the look' from the priest when I told him I had nothing to confess. He insisted that I did, so I made something up. How fucked up is that? I felt so guilty about it that I told him about the lie at my next confession. I thought he was going to stroke out and die and then I'd have to confess the murder at the next confession, or I'd possibly have a good story to tell the Devil when I arrived in Hell, which at the very least would be my punishment.

The Devil was a very frightening thing to Catholics. I remember seeing *The Exorcist* and decades later it still creeps me out when I hear "Tubular Bells". One night while driving home from a shopping sortie with my sister, I did my best possessed Linda Blair impression, complete with demonic growling and snickering. Instead of the words from the movie, "Your mother sucks cocks in Hell," I snarled, "Your mother combs her hair with buttered toast." Funny stuff among my friends but not so funny to my sister who slapped me and threated to make me walk home if I continued.

I also recall getting the strap from the nuns when I was in grade 2 along with five other children. We were guilty of making faces at each other and laughing in church. Sheesh! We were six or seven years old. We are supposed to make faces at each other and laugh in church. Lighten up, (Sister Mary) Francis!

I also remember a grade 4 teacher who made us kneel on unpopped corn. We girls had to wear skirts and knee socks (and no patent leather shoes cause the boys could see 'stuff' in the reflection!)

I remember going home with dents in my bare knees from the corn, but it was better than when that same teacher made us eat pepper for saying something heathenesque. Gotta love Catholic school, but you did have incentive to learn and behave most of the time.

Inner voice: Been to confession lately? Snicker...

Furiosa: THE POWER OF CHRIST COMPELS YOU! THE POWER OF CHRIST COMPELS YOU!

She Devils

Speaking of evil, what kind of fresh Hell is today's faux feminist fuckery?

I find it sad that today's feminists push victimhood as the goal and beating down men as a way of lifting women up. That doesn't work. They weaponize victimhood and proclaim that to be the most empowered person you must be the weakest one in the safe space with the most real or imagined oppressors keeping you down. The truth is you are the only one keeping you down. To demand special treatment at the expense of others under the guise of equality is madness. To have politicians say you are equal but just not equal enough to succeed without the help of Uncle Sugar is soul- and potential-crushing. A quick look around at the most successful minorities and women tells me they didn't get there by whining, taking a government handout, or taking advantage of quotas. They worked their asses off.

I am not a feminist by today's standards because I don't believe women need to emasculate men or bring them down a peg to ensure woman will succeed. I'm not competing against them or other women for that matter. I am doing what I do and trying to be the best I can be, not just as good as the next person, male or female. I certainly don't want to demand they give me special treatment merely because I have a vagina. I want to succeed because of the work I put out there, and not merely because I am female. I find that insulting and demeaning. I don't know what today's feminists are fighting for and when asked many of them don't seem to know either.

I'm also waiting for the backlash against transgenders who are kicking ass in women's and girls' sports. Haven't heard any complaints about those who were born men and are now identifying as women appropriating the female sex. In time, they will wipe out cis-gendered women's and girls' sports completely. I cannot wait to see Serena Williams or Megan Rapinoe lose to a man who has decided to be a female athlete. I'll order in extra popcorn to see that show. Martina Navratilova had to apologize for implying that transgenders were cheating because they were biological males competing against females. Giving in to bullies is not the way to stand up for women's and girls' rights.

As we headed into the 2020 election in the USA, and so-called feminists ignored the sexual assault claims against Joe Biden. I wondered what happened to #MeToo and Hillary Clinton saying, "All women must be believed." Clinton saying that was laughable since her own husband was accused of rape and sexual assault by many women and Hillary absolutely shredded those women in public.

As Dana Perino put it, "The bigger picture is that the #MeToo movement has collapsed under the weight of the Democrats' hypocrisy, but that will be the consequence that they face."

For some reason feminists have equated being equal to men as taking on the worst traits associated with men, like anger, violence, aggressiveness, crudeness, vulgarity, and hyper competitiveness while eschewing their femininity. They blame men for their failure to succeed and scream about toxic masculinity, patriarchy, and white male privilege. I see women marching in the streets shirtless or wearing only bras and shorts. They have painted SLUT on their bare stomachs, or they have gone all out and strapped mattresses to their backs. They put on vagina costumes and pink pussy hats, and off they go, shrieking and howling at the sky, limbs flailing and arms akimbo.

At the same time, they complain how unfair it is that no one takes them seriously and that they get no respect. Behaviour of this type used to get one taken in for a mental health evaluation, and it does nothing to raise women up.

I think today's feminists have fucked up the progress the first and second wave feminists made. This latest wave is more like a flaming tsunami of seething hatred for all things male, all things feminine, and all things having to do with traditional family values. I don't see how they are lifting women up. Their well-intentioned #MeToo movement is stopping male and female business owners from hiring qualified women in fear that maybe ten weeks or ten years from now if that woman is passed up for a promotion she feels she deserves, she might bring down the business and some people's lives and careers by screaming #MeToo! I don't blame business owners for being cautious. Thanks, Feminists! Love ya'! When I see the feminists marching for women's rights we already have and acting the way they do, I don't know whether to laugh or just scream until my eyes bleed.

Even James Brown knows it's a man's world, but it's nothing without a woman in it. It's a man's world, until it isn't. I think it's because of the recent women's movement that I notice some men will look at me for a second before opening a door for me. They need to assess whether I will rip their faces off for their merely being polite. I, of course, smile, and I have even opened doors for men entering a building if their arms are full or if I get there first and they are close behind. It's just common courtesy. Some women just look for an excuse to be offended by a horrible misogynist that dares to open the door for them or worse, if the vile beast should compliment them on their appearance. That is, in their view, akin to raping them with their eyes.

These are the same women who sit home Saturday nights with their six cats, shoveling Ben & Jerry's Chunky Monkey ice cream straight from the bucket into their pie holes while complaining that there are no real men around anymore.

Frankly, I find what today's feminists call toxic masculinity very intoxicating. I am repulsed by the pathologically apologetic, soy boy beta manlets pretending to be supporters of women's rights just so they can get laid. I don't believe you ever raise yourself up by trying to knock someone else down, and I believe in commanding respect, not demanding it.

Men and women are not equal, and one is not superior to the other. Women were not created to do the things that men can do. They were created to do the things men cannot do. Masculinity is not toxic, and besides, I believe femininity is much more powerful. It's not my fault today's feminists don't get that and feel they need to deny part of who they are. Women can be powerful and feminine. Men and women are different. Who knew? Viva la difference!

Inner voice: You should check your cis-gendered privilege.

Furiosa: It puts the cis-gendered snowflake speak in the basket or it gets the hose again.

Food for the soul

I've never read the *Chicken Soup for the Soul* books, but I keep getting the author's emails so I'm gonna check them out one day.

Chicken soup is nice, but my soul wants lobster bisque.

My soul wants crab cakes, crème brûlée and wine.

My soul wants to laugh and cry till it shakes.

My soul wants to sing, dance, and make love.

Feed my soul, damn it, but bring more than chicken soup. Make it a big old bowl of black bean soup, a side of fried plantains, and a Cuban sammich.

Find what feeds your soul. For me, it's a star-filled sky, a secluded beach in any season, a good book, and a warm blanket by the fire, delicious food shared with friends and, depending on the day and who I'm with and where I am, I love music and lots of noise, but I also adore total silence, which is highly underrated. Always good is a day spent with no phones, no TV, and no electronic distractions, the farther away from people and buildings and highways the better. All splendid stuff. All food for my soul.

Stargazing

"Oh, how you shine with your heart full of moonlight and your soul full of stars,

You have the wisdom, the love, and the courage,

Be still and listen—your soul already knows."

—Unknown Author

Have you ever listened to the stars in the sky? Sure, we can see them and they're beautiful, but have you ever listened to them? Imagine a beachside cottage porch chockablock with brass windchimes during a turbulent and wildly windy summer storm, and that is how loudly the stars speak to me. The stars do sing out in an otherworldly and beautiful roar that you will hear with your eyes and all of your senses, really, but only if you truly listen. They shine and twinkle for you and for me.

I am out every night just before sleep star-gazing and enjoying Mother Nature's concert, even in winter. From my balcony I look up at the stars and think of my dear friends scattered across the planet, and I smile because I know they are under the same sky and stars as I am, so they really aren't so far away at all.

Unfortunately, I cannot see many stars most nights because the light pollution from the concrete jungle I live in swallows them up. On a good night, I see 30 stars. One evening while driving the overseas highway from Miami to Key West at midnight, I looked up and was gobsmacked by the number of and the blinding brilliance of the stars. I had forgotten how the night sky looked, and I actually teared up at the sight of it. I don't know where my tears ended and the stars' light began. I hadn't seen that since I was a child camping in a remote area. It planted a seed in my heart to find a place to go where I could see even more stars. I was on a mission and after coming across a fantastic documentary called *Cielo* about the scientists studying the skies in Chile, I knew I had found that place. Within six months I was on a plane by myself and headed eventually to the Atacama Desert.

Once you are in Santiago, you take a two-hour plane ride to Calama and from there it's another one-and-a-half-hour car ride further into the desert. San Padro de Atacama has one of the darkest skies free of light pollution on the planet. Astronomers go there to do their best work. I met up with a group of five other travellers from across the world, and I told them I was going to a stargazing event that night and, of course, they all wanted to go. It was even better than I anticipated. The Milky Way was so close you could almost touch it, and it definitely touched all of us.

I am quite sure that if everyone went outside and looked at the sky every day, either to watch a sunrise or a sunset or to look at the stars, it would change their perspective on life. The chaotic cities we live in suffocate our souls and our connection to nature. We all need to escape to the woods, the ocean, or the desert to reconnect with and heal ourselves. It calms the mind and slows or stops the constant negative chatter of the inner voice that keeps us from being truly at peace. Just as unplugging or turning off a computer or phone resets it, unplugging ourselves from the rat race and technology does wonders for our body and mind. It's not selfish. If you can steal away 20 minutes a day, even to a quiet room in your house, to shut out the cacophonous hurly-burly of the concrete jungle, you will find a chunk of peace that will feed your soul what it needs. It will change you forever.

> **"It's wonderful to spend time in places where there is no civilization. You always feel more civilized when you return."**
>
> —**Furiosa**

15

Into the Depths

Oceans call me. I close my eyes right now and I can hear the soothing sounds of the water rolling and splashing onto the powdery sand that begs to cover my toes. The water's call is incessant. I go to it as often as I can, and when I get there, I know I am as at home as I am under the Milky Way in Chile. As I walk toward the water, a sense of peace washes over me before the waves do. As I enter the water, I feel I am part of the living planet, and the city sludge is washed out of every part of my mind, body, and soul. I am quite certain I was a mermaid in a prior life. They're fascinating creatures, really.

> **"When mermaids lie around in the water they are 'majestic' and 'so beautiful' but when I do it, I'm 'a drunk' and 'banned from the aquarium'."**
>
> —Unknown author

Inner Voice: Mermaid my ass! You left out one teeny weeny tiny detail. You cannot swim worth a shit. Do I need to remind you of the paddleboard fiasco?

Furiosa: Quit clouding the issue with pesky facts and stuff! You're harshing my mermaid mellow.

16

Dorian Gray

My favorite book is *Dorian Gray* by Oscar Wilde. Some people wear their *Dorian Gray* portrait on their face. The older we get, the more our physical beauty softens and fades, so we better have worked on our inner beauty, which is ultimately the most important, valuable, and enduring of the two. We fight to maintain our outer appearance with expensive lotions and potions and even going under the knife, which rarely works out well, in my opinion. We always want to have an enticing wrapper but not worry about what is underneath. Work on patience, gratitude, kindness, and giving and receiving love. Be kind and try listening more and talking less. Give to those who need it but can give you nothing back and you will receive much more in return. You will understand this when you give of yourself without expecting anything or keeping score. Easier said than done, but trust me, it is the truth. The times I have given someone something—something that I could not afford to give, but to someone who needed it more—I always received as much or more in return from the most surprising places.

Some people are nice to look at but ugly to the bone on the inside, and they poison your space when you are near them. I despise when I or someone else is bubbling over with happiness or good news and some negative dullard tries to squash that joy. Negativity really irritates me and puts a knot in my stomach. I immediately remove myself from that person's presence. Life is too short. People like that just need a big hug… with a woodchipper. In this case, I am happy to oblige as I don't use it often but my verbal woodchipper is always at the ready should they persist and I should I find a chop or two from my verbal axe isn't doing the job.

17

Superpowers

I have a natural gift, a superpower, if you will, for being able to verbally whack people in half. I can dish out psyche-crushing sarcasm better than most. I'll throw out acerbic insults like a lidless popcorn maker if I feel I or my friends are being wrongfully attacked. I prefer doing that to punching someone because mental abuse is less messy, and it lasts longer. It has to be verbal because I certainly can't be chipping my manicure or splashing blood on my Louboutins. Though it doesn't sound like it, lately I have been trying to project positivity and joy, and I try not to lash out unless someone is bothering me or my loved ones or is just being mean and nasty and clearly inserting themselves into a room or conversation to provoke a reaction and hurt someone. Crybullies, those who bully people and then cry when their victims return fire, are very weak and don't need more than a few good one-liners lobbed at them. Rarely is a full verbal beat down necessary and it should not be wasted on a common troll and/or the willfully ignorant, although I might do it anyway because it can be fun. Again, I am a bitch that way. Choose your battles carefully, though, as bullies are a stupid lot and most are not worth your time, especially if you run into one of the unstable ones.

18

Mess is a matter of perspective

They say the inside of your purse and your home are the reflection of your mind and how you live your life. Let's not discuss the inside of my purse. I need everything in it… or I will eventually. I'm just happy when it passes airport security.

I love having everything in its place, but I certainly don't fret none about a sweater thrown over a chair or stacks of books piling up beside my bed. My house is uncluttered and very clean, but I do have one clothes closet I am afraid to get to the back of in case a body turns up in there. I guess I'll wait until the cast of *Hoarders* shows up. That might motivate me. I am in the process of throwing things out and giving things away and it feels good to lighten up a little. I will get to the purse(s) eventually.

Inner Voice: Do you need that 2016 Steven Tyler concert ticket stub or those eight hair ties? And how old is that chocolate raisin protein bar? Did it have raisins in it when you first put it in your purse and why are they moving? Ewwwww!

Furiosa: HEY! It's blasphemy to throw out a Steven Fuckin' Tyler anything!

Inner Voice

If your inner voice had a face, you would punch it

It almost never shuts up
It chains you to a reality that is defined by someone else
It filters your beliefs
It keeps you in your limited safety zone

It keeps you uncomfortably comfortable in a state of inaction, but to grow and learn you have to step out of the comfort zone. You have to be uncomfortable and push past it.

It is better to regret what you did than to regret what you didn't do because you were afraid. If you aren't afraid once in a while, you're not challenging yourself and you're not growing.

Sometimes you have to shut off the voice in your head and listen to your heart. Do not let your inner voice talk to you in a manner you would not use with your loved ones in or in a way that you would not accept from someone else.

Inner voice: I am reality, Sugar. Maybe they should learn to deal with reality.

Furiosa: Maybe they don't want to be chained to a reality whose limits are set by someone else! We already covered this. Try to keep up, Sugar!

Power of Silence

"Silence is one of the great arts of conversation"

—Marcus Tullius Cicero

I can now say I am fluent in the language of silence.

This is so true. I believe you can say more with silence than with words, and the only time I've experienced an awkward silence is when a lie has been told or someone is being mean.

Silence can be weaponized to punish someone, or it can be a good thing used to protect someone from hurt. The loudest screams of either joyous amazement or darkest despair come from those who remain silent.

Let's talk about good silence. Nothing is as loud as life and nature rushing into your body to fill the void left in a silent space. At first, it is a little unnerving but if you let it happen, the voices in your head stop chattering and your thoughts stop swirling and distracting you from the present moment. Calm and peace emerge, and time seems to slow or stop. You are in touch with every fiber of your being.

If you don't get the magnificence of a roaring silence, skip this paragraph. Hopefully in the future you will come to understand it and you will see how much humans need it to recharge. You won't be able to live without it, and then you will make time each day to experience it. Whether you have a quiet space in your house or you can get away to the woods or to a deserted beach, it is as essential to your mind and soul as food is to your body.

For now, if you don't get it, it's me, it's not you. Yeah! That's it! It's me… snicker.

Inner voice: It's definitely you… snicker.

Furiosa: We're talking about silence. How about you try some?

21

Planet Furiosa

I spend hours at the lake each winter, bundled in my raccoon coat and braving the biting wind to take in one of the most beautiful sights in the world—a lake that is frozen as far as the eye can see. It looks like another world, and it is all mine. On the deserted beach, with my back to the cottages, it seems like I am the only one on the planet. On Planet Furiosa there is only the sound of the wind whipping to and fro, occasionally sending a spray of powdery snow from one drift to another. Everything is frozen winter white right up to where the shock of sky-blue patches begin and a blazing orange fireball punches holes into the clouds sending rays of blinding sunshine dancing down onto the ice and snow.

Alone, but certainly not lonely, I breathe in every iota of my very own planet and my mind empties and calms sharpish. My inner voice, for once in its life, shuts the fuck up. It, too, is joyously gobsmacked by Mother Nature's precious displays on our visits to the beach. Peace and bliss enter every cell of my body and mind. That, too, is my food for the soul.

22

Beautiful noise

As beautiful as silence is, there are sounds that are equally as beautiful.

Slow, rolling ocean waves gently kissing the thirsty sand sometimes gifting it with pretty shells and those rare chunks of white, blue, and green sea glass.

Turbulent ocean waves crashing on shore during a thunder and lightning storm.

The crunching of freshly fallen snow under your boots as you walk on a still and starry winter night.

The sound of my footsteps walking away from someone who doesn't deserve me.

A spoon cracking the burnt sugar crust on a perfect crème brûlée.

A spoon cracking the burnt sugar crust on a perfect crème brûlée.

Inner voice: Idiot! Have you been drinking? You said 'a spoon cracking the burnt sugar crust on a perfect crème brûlée' twice.

Furiosa: I am aware, Miss Thing! I love crème brûlée. I don't ever remember eating just one, hence it bears repeating. Yum! Yum! Get me some!

23

Let It Go

Things that are certain and that piss me off.

You cannot hang on to some things no matter how tightly you are grasping. You have to let some things go.

Okay! This is huge! On being lonely and alone. There is a difference, and you should appreciate it. When I finally embraced being alone and enjoying it, suddenly everyone wanted to be with me, and I had a hard time ditching people while trying not to hurt their feelings. WTF is up with that? That is a rhetorical question. I do indeed know WTF is up with that and could fill a book with it, but I digress. I guess I'm just pissed it took me so long to figure it out.

Unkind people piss me off.

People that ghost or most people. See rant #25.

People obsessed with likes and upvotes in the online zoo. I never understood why they believe it matters.

Empty crème brûlée ramekins. Grrrrrrrrrrrrrrrrrr!

24

Be brave

When was the last time you did something for the first time?

Think! When was the last time you did something for the first time? It's been a while, hasn't it? So, go do something new already!

I am constantly looking for new things to do for the first time. Right now, I am writing a book for the first time and getting it published.

My favorite first time thing that I did was travel alone. When I go, I go big. I have always had a desire in my heart to go to Israel, and for about a decade people kept telling me they would go with me—next year, next year, next year, or they would say we'll go when it settles down over there.

I decided that things were never going to settle down over there or anywhere else. I told my friends I was going *this* year. "Sure, sure," they said with the expected eye rolls and the 'there she goes again' smirks to go with. I booked the trip and arranged to meet up with a tour group in Tel Aviv, which is exactly what I did. My friends were in shock as they dropped me off at the airport. I think they expected me to turn around and say it was an early April Fools' joke.

I boarded the plane and took my seat, my three seats, actually. I had paid for extra leg room seats since it was a 12-hour flight and luckily had no one beside me. YES! YES! YES! Then they announced we were taking off and it hit me. OMG! I started internally freaking out. What the Hell am I doing? A woman travelling alone to Israel? I had done extensive research about the trip and the country, but I had never travelled so far before and certainly not by myself. I ordered a CC and ginger and watched a movie (*Zero Dark Thirty*), read, ate, binged on gin gin candies until my mouth felt like it was on fire, and then repeated as necessary. It wasn't long and I was thoroughly enjoying the fact that I had 12 hours by myself for the first time in a long time. Bliss and absolute Heaven. No phone, no internet, no nuttin'! This was the beginning of my love of silence and me time. The trip was so epic I went back two years later, and yes, getting there was half the fun.

Ghosting and mosting

Ghosting and mosting or Sugar Pants leaves a mark but not a scar:

This is weaponized silence and can be used to squash trolls or intentionally or unintentionally inflict pain on decent people when it is the choice of cowards and immature faux alphas. We've all used the silent treatment on idiots. Instead of engaging a troll who has just popped up on a thread of comments to disrupt and attack, we have totally ignored them if they are not banned right away. You take away their audience and they move on to get their negative attention fix elsewhere. That's not what I'm talking about here.

Let me define:

Ghosting: The practice of ending a personal relationship, a friendship with someone by suddenly and without explanation withdrawing from all communication.

Mosting: Making extreme declarations of admiration to someone you are dating before cutting contact. (e.g.: Someone says, "I love, adore, crave you! I'm in love with you and I cannot live without you!") and then cuts off all communication with no explanation or warning.

My experience is with ghosting. What I am talking about is someone you build a friendship and connect with over a long period of time on social media, even speaking by private email and telephone and sharing personal details of your offline life. I do this with very few people but when I do I trust them totally. I rarely let my walls down and unfortunately, as I mentioned previously, that leaves me open to being burned on those rare occasions. I totally own that I put myself in that position. Because my judgement has been 99% correct and I have met some wonderful and true friends, I accept the risk.

You cannot meet amazing people without opening your heart and trusting once in a while. You take a chance that someone will rip it out of your chest and stomp on it, but I am willing to take that chance since it doesn't happen often and it's not like I don't have warnings. I sometimes hope to wait people out while they struggle to become what they are meant to be. I became close friends with someone I have known a couple of years. Let's call him Sugar Pants. We confided in each other, and I thought we had a special friendship that would last forever. It was not to be.

Without warning, and without any argument or disagreement, after talking every day sometimes for hours off and on, he suddenly stopped talking to me. A wall of silence. That's fine. We all need to be left alone and have some space to ourselves, but we're usually respectful enough to reply to our friends when they ask if we're okay. I got dead silence, though I saw him furiously chatting up a storm on the internet. I could always tell when something was wrong by the content and tone of his online posts. That's another thread for another day cause Lawdy! Ain't nobody got time for that in this book! Broken people are so predictable once you know them. I speak from experience as a broken person, but I digress.

I really wished this person no harm. I knew their life struggles (which we all have) and I didn't want to add to them. I even wished him well and though I am not an overly religious person I said I would pray for him. I try hard to understand people's motives for doing things. I have great empathy for people. The motives may seem totally fucked up and illogical, but I do see how they got there. That doesn't mean I like it and it doesn't excuse their atrocious behaviour, but I get it. I can't fix them, though naively I try. They have to work on those things themselves. I will not be a doormat, and I have my own issues I'm working on.

He remained silent for five months and I didn't think much about him until he contacted me with a sheepish email. We started chatting again and resumed the friendship… yada yada yada, a month later he bugged out again. I asked him to at least acknowledge that there was a human being on the other side of his computer and told him he should say goodbye instead of being a coward. Again, I saw him chatting all over the interwebs, a pathetic cry for help of sorts. Sorry! Not sorry! My self-respect kicked in big time. I ripped him another one in an email, and he let loose with a crap load of hysterical hyperbolic hooey and somehow turned it around to be my fault for making him mad because I demanded a respectful acknowledgement.

I told him I was not a computer app he could use when he wanted and then turn off until next time. I am a real live person and I thought I was his friend. You've confused me with somebody else, Sugar Pants! Furiosa snaps her fingers over Sugar Pants' head!

Thank God I have been given the grace to see that it wasn't me, even though he tried his hardest to gaslight me to convince himself, I suppose. It's him and I can do nothing but wish him well and move on.

I am an observer of people and a writer. I have been on social media for a decade and have seen a lot. I have evolved, and I have grown for the better. I have witnessed many cruel things that people have said and done to others. The obvious stalkers and trolls and their vulgar insults are one thing but ghosting and mosting are the worst in my opinion. I think these behaviours are cowardly, small, and evil. Women do it too, but usually it is men who pretend to be alpha males and when it comes down to it, they cannot even tell a woman they don't want to be friends or partners any more. It's really a blessing for the man or woman who gets ghosted, and it's understandable to be confused and angry. But we should all look for the silver lining when someone acts in a willfully disrespectful and dishonest manner. This person is playing the part of the person they want to be and or the person they think others want them to be. Walk away quickly if they do not own their behaviour and change it. They know very well that what they are doing will hurt someone and they selfishly do it anyway. They think it will save them from being hurt by facing the truth of their inability to man up or woman up, as the case may be. They cannot function in an adult relationship, whether it be a friendship or a romantic one, and so they need to be gone.

I am not in the habit of bringing my personal shit out in public, but at this point in my life I do not worry about sharing my feeling and thoughts. I am human and I am not the only person going through these things. That is the point: we go through them. We don't wallow in them. We learn from them and move on. I write mostly from the heart while using my head just a little, all the while arguing and negotiating with my inner voice. I want to inspire people and make them think and feel things and be encouraged to be themselves.

Social media is so damned impersonal, and I hate that part of it. I try to bring a little heart, soul, and humour into the mix. These are things that are so lacking in this graceless age in which we live. The internet is not real, and some people think this gives them the right to treat the person on the other side of their screen like crap. I am not having it, and neither should you.

The ghosting and mosting thing hit home for me, and I see it happening all over to many people. Social media is also used by all kinds of predators who look for people with good hearts and gentle souls so they can squash them for their sick pleasure. I am a very kind person and do not go out of my way to hurt people. I stick up for people that are down and being picked on, but don't you ever mistake my friendly demeanor for weakness because I have no trouble tossing you into the verbal woodchipper in an instant. I can take care of myself, thank you very much. I just don't think most nasty people are worth giving the time of day. I've been on the internet a long time, and I have been observing some people from a distance and others from close up. It's been fascinating. This book came from those experiences, but I do not name names. It isn't necessary, and that's not how I roll.

In closing, I wish the ghoster/moster, who I am sure is reading this, all the best, and I ask that he try to be kinder to the next person because they might be a fire starter or a stabber—see rant #33. LOL.

Inner voice: I told you he was broken.

Furiosa: We're all broken.

Inner voice: I'm not broken.

Furiosa: Only because I can't find your face.

26

Deal with it, whatever it is.

Don't make it worse with quick fixes or by numbing the pain.

Whatever you do, when you are healing your heart from a loss and/or breakup or are just overwhelmed with life stuff, do not engage in self-destructive behaviour that makes all problems worse. Do constructive things, be good to yourself. Buy yourself flowers and take bubble baths and eat well. Visit good friends and take a walk outside and really appreciate the sun and the wind on your face.

Drowning your sorrows in excessive drinking, drugs, internet, and eating does not work. Be good to yourself. You deserve it. Ask for help. You will be fine. You'll be better than fine. You'll be fabulous!

> **"I tried to drown my sorrows with alcohol, but the bastards could swim."**
>
> —Frida Kahlo

> **"I tried to drown my sorrows with alcohol and not only could the bastards swim, but they were also throwing me anchors."**
>
> —Furiosa

27

Take a Leap

I hope you dance. Cross that Rubicon.

This has nothing to do with the conga.

A favorite song is Lee Ann Womack's "I Hope You Dance", and it has nothing to do with the conga, either.

This song is about never taking the easy way out by not acting. Don't sit it out—dance.

I am inviting you to dance. I'm inviting you to cross that Rubicon. Many people look at the things I've done and say they wish they could be me and do what I do. The truth is, they don't want to be me. They want to be themselves. The truth is, they can do what I do but they are standing in their own way. They ask, "Who will let me do that?" when they should be asking, "Who will stop me from doing that?"

They are allowing their inner voice to be the boss of them, just as I had for all those years. I got to the point where I felt like a caged animal and decided to let my inner voice know that I was in control now. She could give me advice and warnings, but she no longer could say negative things about me or determine my limitations. No one should be allowed to say negative things to you that are meant to keep you down. No one. You are good enough, you are amazing, you are well equipped to live your dream and to reach your potential. When one door closes, another one will open or you will open one yourself, even if you have to kick it down. It is your time to dance.

28

Living vs Existing

One of my best friends lived life to its fullest right up until cancer took him in his late 70s. Though he was decades older than me, he had no trouble keeping up with me on a recent ten-day tear through Southeast Florida and the Keys. He took every opportunity to dance, metaphorically speaking, and as I vaguely recall, he even ripped it up on the dance floor a time or two during the trip.

One of my fondest memories is seeing him floating on a huge pink flamingo in a pool at a splendid little Key West hotel on Duval St. Eventually, it overturned and tried to kill him, or so he claims. That I do have pictures of. He got over his brush with death quickly once I ordered him a big old wedge of key lime pie and a glass of vino.

He recently took me old school roller skating, which is something I have not done since I was a teenager. I might add I won't be doing that again anytime soon, even after the bruises heal. By the way, if you don't have pictures of our Florida trip, it never happened.

Inner Voice: I have pictures!

Furiosa: Bitch! Those are Photoshopped! Furiosa bats her eyelashes, throws her head back and laughs uproariously.

29

Social media — the human rock tumbler

Many people on social media live lives of quiet desperation, some not so quiet.

On social media, we are all jaggy, craggy nuggets smashing up against each other, and it's up to you whether you come out of it a polished gem or a pile of crumbled rocks and dust. I choose to be a gem—not perfect, beautifully broken, and fabulously flawed, but a gem, nonetheless.

The last decade I have been on social media, I have been liked, loved, hated, chewed up, spit out, and stomped on—metaphorically speaking, regarding the latter, but that didn't make it hurt any less. At the three-year point I was ready to delete my account like many of my online friends had done after being gang trolled and threatened with doxing. It was mostly people on the uber liberal political sites that were the most vulgar and obnoxious. Backed into a corner, I went into fight mode, and I formed alliances and created private groups where likeminded folks could speak freely and take a breather from the online poo flinging. At the same time, I stumbled onto a music site followed by a pack of trollish jackals, and after the owners did a quick assessment of the verbal melee that had blown up their usually peaceful site, the stalkers were dispatched with haste, and I was welcomed to stay. I have never left the site, and I renewed my love of music, which I had sidelined for too many years. I came out of my self-imposed decade of conformity where I had existed and not lived and during which I listened to very little music and watched very few movies. I feel most of the products coming out of the entertainment industry after the 1980s were crap anyway, but I now wonder how I survived without music, my drug of choice.

I made that music site my home, and I did venture out into the fray once in a while, but I chose my battles more wisely. For the most part, I avoid psychotically negative people, of which there are many. I don't just mean people with different points of view. I am talking about outright dark entities that poison every site they show up on. It is too easy to be pulled down a rabbit hole by these freaks.

"If you want blood, you got it..." This is a great song by AC/DC that describes the chaos of the human zoo in which we live and tells us that to survive you have to fight back sometimes.

Most people on the interwebs live lives of quiet desperation, but others are not so quiet about their desperation, and they want you to be as miserable as they are. I find most of them are looking for something to fill the void in their real lives. Many crave intimacy and human contact but create an unrealistic online persona that makes it impossible to ever follow through on any genuine relationship, should they ever meet up with those they virtually connect with. Gaining real friends on the internet only works out if you are, for the most part, the same person you are online as you are in real life. That leaves out 85% of people. I have been lucky. I have made lifelong friends with some really cool and decent human beings. I tend to be cautious but take people at their word when I do become friends and let the filter down, so of course it follows that I have also been burned badly for seemingly small offenses. This is used as an excuse, I suppose, for chokers who realized their jig was probably just about up. I should be angry, but

I am not. I have grown enough to realize that they are probably mad enough at themselves for both of us. I am sad that they have lived this long and still can't resolve conflicts in an adult way, nor can they accept or give a sincere apology. I suppose the few friends I became very close with who choked and ghosted me couldn't follow through on their promise of honest friendship. I guess they didn't expect me to return their words and really mean them. I don't offer close friendship lightly. I am an extremely emotional and passionate person, but I can also reason and discuss things rationally when I am mad. I am grateful that I have learned that lesson in self-control. I may have to stop having certain people in my life, but I cannot stay angry or seek revenge.

I have finally started seeing the silver lining in things that happened to me, and I am proud of how I handle them most of the time (no one is perfect). I have switched my approach so when disaster hits, I instantly look for a way to fix it, whereas before I would have been overcome with doom and gloom and panic and freeze. People that have screwed me over after I confided in them have made me feel little more than pity for them, whereas before I would have been angry. Because they also confided in me, I can clearly see what made them do it. It's not right, it's not rational, and most times it's a knee-jerk reaction to something that triggered them emotionally. Pride gets in the way after their outbursts, and that puts the kibosh on the friendship. I still offer my friendship, wish them well, and shake my head at the loss for them and for me. How sad that people watch themselves repeating the same actions they know will cause them more suffering and hurt people they love. My offer of friendship and understanding at this point seems to make them react more angrily, even though I know they are sad. True love and friendship should be stronger than pride. Shrugs. I have smashed a lot of my own negative patterns, and I have begun to enjoy the sound of my footsteps running away—or is it skipping away? —from toxic and dark entities and so-called friends that are so bad for me.

I'm not sure who said but is so true:

"To hold anger inside is like drinking poison and expecting the other person to die."

Bitch, please! That is never going to happen. Learn from it, hope the other person eventually finds happiness, be sure to wish them well, and then move on. That will either make them angrier at you for not being mad at them or it will plant a seed of change in them and maybe soften their heart. I have had both effects on people, and both made me smile.

Oscar Wilde said, "Always forgive your enemies, nothing annoys them more."

30

Where the hell are you?

After losing two good friends to cancer in the span of seven months and enduring some other curveballs life throws at us all, and even though I am at a crossroads in my life, I know which direction I am heading and I am in a good place. After a lifetime of being on a rickety rollercoaster of caring and not caring what people think, I have arrived at Don'tLikeMeGoFuckYourselfVille. It is a very good place to be. I do not go out of my way to hurt people, and I don't even waste my time insulting or sawing people in half verbally unless they really deserve it, for example, if they are bothering my friends. I find ignoring people pisses them off more than engaging them in a battle of wits and insults they are clearly ill equipped to fight. I don't have "lastworditis", which is the Achilles heel of most trolls. It is the most debilitating and prevalent disease for trolls on social media. I am comfortable with who I am becoming. I am beautifully broken, and it has made me better. I am flawed but in a fabulous way. I am not perfect, but I am perfectly happy with that fact. I have not finished dancing, and I do not intend to sit it out.

31

Spilled milk is one of the four main food groups

Spilling milk in my house won't get you into trouble but spilling alcoholic beverages may get you thrown into the woodchipper.

Don't do it. Don't cry over spilled milk. Whatever you did is done. If you can fix it, do so. If necessary, apologize and move on. Spilled milk?? Pfffffffffffffttt! It's one of the four main food groups along with chocolate, bacon, and crème brûlée.

So, dry those pretty eyes and pour another glass of milk, a bigger glass. Make it coconut milk, add a big splash of rum, and garnish it with a pineapple spear and a pretty little paper umbrella. Drink up. Life is short.

When you start each day's adventure, it's essential to glance in the rearview mirror but you must look ahead to where you want to go before you hit the gas. Do not keep dwelling on or looking at your past. It's like staring directing at a blazing sun—you will lose your focus and burn your retinas out. A quick glance behind you and then put on some cool shades and floor it!

Past, present, and future.

Stop saying, "I'll be happy when or if_____" (fill in the blank). Choose to be happy now.

You aren't living in the past.

You aren't living in the future.

Make now the best time of your life. Don't miss today because you are looking backward and forward. Learn from the past, plan for the future, but live in this moment.

These *are* the good old days.

Don't look behind you—you're not going that way.

32

Nobody's business but your own

On worrying about what others think

In a word—DON'T!

Most people aren't thinking about you as much as you think they are thinking about you. Most of the time they aren't thinking about you at all. I have had people apologize to me for something they did in the recent past and I have no clue what they are talking about. They claim they said or did something that I may or may not have been offended by. Um... seriously, if I don't recall, it couldn't have offended me much or you just didn't make that big an impression on me. It's okay. Lots of people don't remember me, either. We aren't as important in other people's lives as we think we are, and we will have to get over that. People don't even remember the time you were out for dinner with friends, left your glasses on the table, and walked into the men's washroom by mistake. Okay! Okay! They always remember that kind of shit, at least the guy standing at the urinal when I walked in on him remembers. I turned my embarrassment into his by glancing downwards and saying, "Oh dear! The water in the pool must be very cold today." Then I snickered, clapped imaginary dust off my hands, and went off to find my way to the ladies' room. As he walked past my table a few minutes later, I was so tempted to tell him to try the shrimp special and for dessert the spotted dick, but no sense piling it on.

Pro tip: In the end, we are going to die, and it won't matter. Go for it! People only think about themselves. They may spend a moment pointing out the embarrassing gaffs of others, but they quickly move back to their own thoughts and feelings and worrying about what others are thinking of them. Don't waste time on this trap. What the hell does it matter what people think? It doesn't! It only matters what you think.

It only matters how you see yourself, and you are magnificent!

33

Crazy women and men as victims

We all know men who wear it as a badge of honour that they dated crazy women and the sex was great. This begs the question: Would sex with a non-crazy woman be great if this same man did something different than he is now doing and didn't leave it up to the supposedly crazy woman to make the sex great? LOL… worth considering.

They avoid (akin to ghosting and mosting) the alleged crazy woman and then act surprised and even brag about how angry the woman was afterwards. They even boast that the woman did something like start the man's car on fire or stab him. This is a red flag, ladies, and should tell us that either this man is attracted to crazy, violent women who don't break up well or this man makes women angry enough to commit violent acts. Of course, there is no excuse for stabbing people or starting their cars on fire, but it is understandable that being treated poorly could bring about that much anger in the right person.

It's usually lonely, middle-aged men who are well past their prime who brag about their so-called conquests of attracting lunatics, and you would think these men would have a little self-awareness at their age and think, "Hey! Helga started my car on fire, Big Mama Sally threw my cellphone in the toilet, Sybil stabbed me, and Elly May's on her way over with a gun… Maybe it's something I'm doing?" Duh! At the least, hearing a guy talk like this would help us distinguish between the good crazy and the bad crazy.

These dudes are definitely the bad crazy and should be avoided as potential boyfriends and/or friends.

Dating crazy women says more about the man than it does about the woman. I don't care who people date or become friends with, I just think it's nice if, when you want out of the relationship, you let the other person know, too. Treat all human beings, especially those who are being straight up and honest with you, with respect and dignity. That's not the real world though, and so I rant. Men that are merely using crazy women for sex and stringing them along knowing they will hurt them are driven by their basic instincts and operating on the level of gutter-dwelling knuckle draggers and shaved apes who have no respect for themselves so cannot be expected to have it for others. Best to run away when these dark entities enter your space. Their stories are not even amusing, they are sad. While no one deserves to be violently attacked, these men are fully aware of how to avoid it.

Inner voice: You're a nice girl, you carry an axe... snicker.

Furiosa: Do you want the axe? Cause that's how you get the axe!

34

The filter

Some days my filter is 99% down. I post and say things I would normally edit. Strange, but these are the days my comments and rants get the most positive feedback. Shrugs. So slowly I have just left the filter down and let it rip.

I let the words tumble out, sometimes without thinking, and occasionally they spray out like howitzer shells. As I have said before, in the end it won't matter. I still have enough of a filter up that I don't intentionally hurt people I like with words. I won't waste time on trolls who post only to start an argument. I am proud to say I do not have that horrible affliction most trolls and socially retarded people have—"lastworditis". I can walk away and let them have their precious word, which is usually something akin to "Duh!" Let's face it, these people aren't exactly splitting atoms, and most are unemployed cretins living in mom's basement. They move on quickly with their big 'win' and I am left in peace. That said, I have been known to verbally saw people in half or chop them to pieces with my verbal axe if they are being plain mean, racist, antisemitic, or just plain stupid.

While I don't go out of my way to be obnoxious, there are many people who do, and these are the ones who need the verbal axe.

35

Keeping it real

Who are you when no one is looking?

Kindness, Character, and Reputation

Sometimes a little act of kindness can bring a fellow human being out of the depths of despair or even out of a mild funk. A genuine compliment, a hug, surprising someone with a salted, milk chocolate covered caramel (yes, please!) or a happy face emoji can make their day. One of the nicest things I saw someone do happened on a bus I was on a few years ago. A man with special needs was being mocked and laughed at by some young kids, and you could tell he was uncomfortable. The man sneezed and his nose was running heavily, if you know what I mean. I am ashamed to say I looked away, trying not to show my disgust. The kids sniggered some more but a woman got up, went over to the man, and offered him a Kleenex, which he thanked her for. She told him to keep the whole package and she smiled at him. He beamed radiantly and told her to have a nice day as she gave the sniggering kids 'the look'. The kids shut up and I felt like an ass. The man held his head a little higher. I have helped someone having seizures on a bus once, fending off the vulture who tried to take his wallet claiming he was looking for medical info, but that comes nowhere near what that woman did by offering the man her Kleenex. She helped him preserve his dignity and that is priceless. Everything you need to know about people you can learn while using public transportation and that was a good lesson on small kindnesses meaning so much to another person. ☺ There is an infinite number of small gestures one can make that take little time and cost nothing. Sometimes just a smile and a hello can change someone's day. Character is defined by how you treat the people who can do nothing for you.

John Wooden said, "Be more concerned with your character than your reputation because your character is what you really are while your reputation is merely what others think you are. The true test of a man's character is what he does when no one is watching."

> **"I don't give a damn 'bout my reputation…"**
>
> **—Joan Jett**

Do not assume things about people. You don't know what they are dealing with. Looks are deceiving. Be kind.

36

"Music is my aeroplane..."

—**Red Hot Chili Peppers**

I cannot say enough about music. One or two notes from certain songs can make me cry or make me deliriously happy. Certain tunes are like musical caffeine or a sedative or they can make me want to move by body. I go with it, unless I am alone in public, of course. Most of the time I do control myself, but music is my drug of choice. My taste is, to put it mildly, eclectic. I love everything from Pavarotti to Patti Smith, from Hole to Stones to Nightwish and Bocelli. I am a Tony Joe White and David Bowie freak. After watching Linda Perry's video where she covers Led Zep's "Misty Mountain Hop", I am convinced she is my Spirit Animal. Music can change your mood in an instant… and the best part? No hangover and no bad side effects. Crank it up!

37

Love

Love is what life is all about and there are many types and levels of love. Love brings us our greatest joys and our worst heartaches and anguish. The key is to learn from your mistakes and keep getting right back in there.

Open your heart.

Is your heart open or have you closed it so you don't get hurt? If it is closed, you cannot love completely and you cannot be loved completely. Take a chance. Sure, you might have your heart ripped out of your chest and stomped on, but love is worth it, yes? The last time I was in love and had that happen I just wanted to die. I just knew I couldn't go on without him. It was the end of the world. The worst part was I knew he still loved me too, but I didn't (and still don't) believe I should have to prove I am worthy of a person's love when they are not proving to be worthy of mine.

Do not stick around and let someone take a metaphorical fish gutting knife and use it to make a jagged radish rose of your heart. I have been broken hearted a few times and thought I was never going to be happy again. I thought I couldn't go on living but I did eventually become happy again and I certainly did go on. You will too. Cry for the first week, then get up and start working out, start writing, take a trip to the ocean, get out and live.

<u>You will get through this latest worst day of your life just as you did the last one and just as you will the next one.</u>

Love and hate can be such strong and excruciatingly painful emotions that they at times threaten to consume us and destroy our lives. Perhaps there really is a thin line between them. We are certain we are going to die without that person and yet most of us survive to ask ourselves later, "What the hell was I thinking?" And yes, most of us jump right back into the fire to risk it all because, of course, it is better to have loved and lost than to never have loved at all, or so they say.

You've been burned more than once so should you just avoid love altogether to keep from being hurt again? You can try, but love will get right in your face when you're not looking for it. Reality says you may be hurt but this time, this may be 'the one'—WTF? What's love got to do with reality, anyway? Rip the bandage off, go for it—but keep an eye out for fish gutting knives. Take the chance, love is worth it. Don't stay closed for too long.

Beauty from Ashes, Ashes to Ashes… whatever! A love story.

Malachy and Cora met in a small, pretty park on the banks of the River Kalamazoo. It was love at first site. This beautiful French girl and the dashing young Irish Air Force member married and yada yada yada… They had eight children. That's what you did back then.

I was the third youngest. I had two younger brothers, four older sisters, and one old brother.

Life was noisy and chaotic in our house. It was small and cramped with ten people and only four bedrooms. Back then, affordable housing meant we had the house we could afford because my parents didn't take handouts.

So, to save their sanity and ours, my parents, like my friends' parents, kicked us all out of the house after dinner. We would play and run around until dusk, then mom would holler for us to come take a bath and get ready for bed.

In the winter, we always had a skating rink in the back yard and played hockey. In the summer, the rink was replaced with a garden, which unfortunately was mostly filled with Swiss chard and rhubarb.

Playing outside was not as dangerous as playing in our house. When our family had food fights, it was to the death. I once took a can of cling peaches to the side of the head, just behind my ear, and needed four stitches to close it up. I eventually learned that my wit won most fights with my older siblings—my wit and being fleet of foot.

My parents stayed married until death did they part, because that's how they did it back then. One day, I got a call saying they had both been admitted to the same hospital. We were told mom had congestive heart failure and would not make it through the night. Dad had been diagnosed with lung cancer, which is ironic since he had quit smoking his unfiltered cigarettes decades earlier. He came down with pneumonia when he was 20 and they removed a lung because back then they didn't have the good drugs we have today. The long scar that surgery left, along with the few nearby brown spots, inspired us to call him 'Freckle Back Railroad Track'. Dad continue smoking with one lung for about 30 years. Now, decades later in the hospital with lung cancer, the doctor told him, "When you get stronger, we will give you chemo." Dad replied, "The hell you will." He was ready to go. Dad passed away ten days later, but mom lived another ten years, mostly just to spite the doctors who had all but pronounced her dead.

Mom and Dad wished to be cremated, have their ashes mixed and then sprinkled in the park they had met in all those years ago.

When the time came, five of the eight children met at one sister's house. She had thrown a plastic cloth over her kitchen table and dumped the two bags containing my parents' ashes in the middle of the table. She mixed them together with a spatula and then scooped the ashes into five bags, one for each of us. It was a little unnerving, but it was their wish and now holding our parents in our hands we were off to the park.

It was a beautiful fall day, and 40 minutes after we arrived at the park, the sun even came out. To cut the tension I made a joke. I turned to everyone and said, "Don't leave Seamus and Poopsie in the car now." We all burst out laughing. Until then we had forgotten about the nicknames our parents had for each other. We were still laughing when someone mentioned that the dearly departed sometimes send signals and messages to you and suggested we should look for these messages as we carried out our parents' wish. We continued to make jokes and watch and listen for signals and messages from Poopsie and Seamus as we spread their ashes along the river's edge. After taking a little time to enjoy the crisp fall air, the view of the water, and the dappled sunlight on the grass beneath the trees, we made our way back to the car.

We hadn't even turned out of the parking lot when we smelled it. Four out of the five of us had stepped in dog droppings and the whole car reeked of it. We bailed out and cleaned our boots and shoes off the best we could with empty plastic bags and napkins. The sister who had mentioned signals and messages and, by the way, the only one without dog doo on her shoes, said she'd warned us. She still claims that Poopsie, my mom, was the culprit, getting back at us for joking about the nicknames she and Dad had shared. She was probably looking down on us and laughing her head off. It's a beautiful thing that Seamus and Poopsie are together again in the park they had met in—unless it is illegal for us to spread ashes in a public park, in which case, it didn't happen.

38

Twin Flames

He knocked softly on the door, whispering "Hello" sweetly as she opened it a crack to see who was there.

Their words danced back and forth, hearts beating faster a white-hot flame appeared promising sweet and lovely things

She, breathless as he, proclaiming adoration, love, and craving kicked down the door she had kept locked for so long

The flames engulfed them and the intensity at once enchanted and terrified him, so he ran away.

He had smashed her filter into a million jagged pieces that would cut them both.

Sometimes you meet your twin flame, and those flames turn into smoldering embers and you both experience a deeper kind of love. Other times, the fire is so intense that it consumes all, leaving just a pile of ashes that eventually are blown away by a bitter wind.

Most of us have been scorched and wondered how in the hell we are ever going to go on without that person... but we did go on, didn't we? We might have even looked back and wondered, "What the fuck was I thinking?" Best to learn the lesson and laugh at ourselves. Lost love is another one of those 'don't look in the rear-view mirror because you're not going that way' thingies.

Inner voice: Ha ha ha ha! Drama Queen Alert! Now you're a poet. This is getting embarrassing.

Furiosa: I don't know what makes one a poet. I'm just splattering words and thoughts on a paper canvas. Do you have a problem with that?

Inner voice: OMG! First a writer and now a poet. Your attempt at poetry is to laugh. I'm just playing devil's advocate, so you don't make a fool of yourself, yet again.

Furiosa: Devil's advocate? More like Devil's wiz.

Inner voice: Will you be an artist next? Paint us a masterpiece? Ha ha and a big fat HA!

Furiosa: Yes, for my first work, I will paint you, right after I draw a chalk outline around your body.

39

Revenge

My comments on love aside, there are still those who feel the need to get back at those who did them wrong in some way. I keep seeing stories where a girl gets dumped and gets revenge on her ex by sleeping with the ex's best friend, brother, sister… whoever! I don't get it at all.

I suggest, while not condoning of course, the following instead:

- Cut the crotches out of all of his underwear and pants—an oldie but a goodie
- Write his phone number and a comment about his liking bears, vinyl, furries, and otherkins in a bunch of men's or gender-neutral bathrooms.
- Hide chunks of raw fish in his curtain rods and heating vents. Bonus if he owns cats, as they will shred the fuck out of his curtains climbing up to get the fetid, festering fish.
- Send any nude pics or sexting messages he sent you to his mom, his aunt, his priest, and boss.
- Limburger cheese in his car engine is good, too.

Leave your mark

Stop trying to be normal. Instead of trying to fit in like a round peg into a square hole, make your own place in the world and invite others to join you. Competing with others squashes your potential and creativity and snuffs out your spirit. Create your own work and don't settle for trying to make their work better. Make yours the best it can be and aim higher. Try. Fail. Try again. If you aren't falling down once in a while, you're not trying hard enough. Getting back up gets easier each time, and you will move forward and grow. Use your inner voice as a guide but do not let it set your limits.

You will not succeed by competing, you will succeed by creating. Do not let others define your success, because success isn't doing better than someone else, it is doing the best you can do. Success is what you say it is. The only limits are the ones you impose on yourself. When you compete with others, you lose your own special mark you can leave with your accomplishments. Your creativity is constrained by focusing on what you feel others might create rather than what you can create on your own, free from outside influence. Unnecessary comparison and competition also provoke animosity toward and from people who could be helpful to you. Be yourself always because you are unique and that is your superpower.

Gratitude – grab some

At this moment, someone is praying for what you take for granted. You once prayed for what you have now.

We tend to focus on what we don't have without appreciating the things we do have. That is wrong and always disappointing. I find when I take stock of the fabulous things I have been blessed with, and there are many, and notice how I have taken those things for granted, I get a beatdown from my guardian angels who mock me mercilessly.

A story if I may? The first time I was told I needed to wear glasses for distance I was so depressed. *I'm not old*, I thought. *Why me? Oh! The horror! My life is over.* The things going on in my pretty little self-absorbed head were absurd, looking back. This was a few years ago when I still risked my mental and physical wellbeing by taking public transportation. I sat on the bus devastated and feeling sorry for myself, barely looking out the window and not caring if I even got off at the right stop because after all, I was now a four-eyes, a specky, a Poindexter, a geek. Grrrrrrrrrrrrrrrrrrr!

The bus lurched on, stopping too often for my liking to pick up more of the unwashed masses. One stop in particular was hacking me off. What the fuck was taking so long to get on the bus? *Probably some drunk old fat fuck*, I thought to myself. *He better not sit next to me reeking of cheap booze and yesterday's tobacco and piss.* The door was open, it was winter, and this four-eyes was shivering.

Get on the damn bus already! Then I saw a furry head and paws come up the stairs followed by…YEP! You guessed it—a blind man. I looked up to the sky and said, "Well played, angels. Good one!" So, I am grateful for my vision, and I must say I have some pretty fly glasses. Some snappy Ray-Ban tortoise shell Clubmasters and some sweet Tiffany & Co. and Dolce & Gabbanas snagged online for a quarter of what they are in the store.

Some of things we take for granted are things we have prayed for in the past. Someone is praying for those things right now. Be grateful.

Inner voice: Um, it's probably illegal to buy those online. They might be stolen or just knock-offs, but it's still wrong.

Furiosa: Yeah, I meant someone else bought those online. Yes, yes, that's it… someone else did—probably that blind dude on the bus.

42

Lab Rat

I'd be remiss if I didn't mention the pandemic. I dragged my feet for two years writing this book. Then came 2020. Another year was added to that because when I came back from Orlando in January 2020, I soon fell very ill with a 'flu'. I went to see a doctor at the end of February, since I still had a cough. I was able to get in to see the doctor because they were only concerned with people who had been to China at that time, so they assumed I was not infected with covid. I was given inhalers and after taking them a month or so I was getting worse, and I couldn't breathe well. But at this time, I could not see a doc in person because it was the beginning of April and they were freaked out about anyone who had travelled anywhere and had a cough. My doctor talked to me over the phone, and at the time I could not go get a test because I didn't have enough symptoms for a referral, and unless I proved I was negative, I couldn't come to her office. I didn't want a test anyway because if you were well enough to go for a test and were positive, they didn't treat you. They just told you to quarantine for 14 days and monitor yourself for worsening symptoms. The doctor prescribed more inhalers. This went on until October and I was hardly able to speak a full sentence without taking extra breaths in between words. I called doc and said someone actually has to see me in person and listen to my lungs and chest up close. I was getting worried, since my dad died of lung cancer and I had had a cough for ten months, not to mention there was a pandemic plus the cold and flu season was coming. She said I had walking pneumonia and prescribed antibiotics over the phone. Normally

I would refuse them, but I had never been this sick for so long. She also said I had to get a negative covid test before I could come into the office the following week. It took me two days to do that, and once I did, there weren't enough tests for them to give me. My heart and lungs and blood were checked, and all were clear, thank God. The drugs worked within five days, but it still took me another four months to get my breathing back to normal. My book sat for the last year because all my effort went into dragging myself to work every day and then back home again. Fortunately, I work in an office by myself 95% of the time.

From the beginning of the lockdowns, I have worked five days a week and usually go for groceries two times a week. In March, I went to Costco and there were no clear signs indicating where people should line up to pay, just masking tape on the floor. I assume it was at least six feet apart.

The guy barked at me to put my feet on the gray tape and my front basket wheels on the next line on the floor.

There was more barking when I didn't stand in the right spot to pay.

A girl with gloves on mauled everyone's groceries and then mine.

More barking to move along and wait for the cart to be loaded after more food mauling.

This reminded me of the "Soup Nazi" episode on *Seinfeld*. I decided to avoid Costco for a few months.

Everything was closed except essential services, you know, like coffee drive thru, McDonald's, liquor stores, and marijuana shops. Really? This is how we know something is wrong in this pandemic.

They announced the number of new cases daily, providing drastically higher numbers than those who were actually sick with it.

Now, we're a year and a half into it and they're pushing the emergency use experimental vaccine thingies on us and telling us we're not getting freedom back until we comply. The field hospitals sitting empty since March 2020 are now jab stations. Not sure what happened to my body, my choice, but I digress.

The really annoying thing is the experts coming on TV every day to drone on about hand washing, social distancing, blah blah blah… nagging *ad nauseum*. They speak slowly to us like we are three years old or mentally deficient. Their models have never been correct. They seem sad that their estimates were wrong and millions didn't die, but they sure get excited when they discuss the data they are collecting on us.

We are told the number of minutes and hours we are spending:

- eating
- watching TV
- reading
- exercising
- having sex
- talking on phone
- shopping online
- working
- eating crème brûlée

This makes me so angry I turn the TV off.

Inner voice: Would you like some cheese with that whine?

Furiosa: *%$#@#!!! I AM NOT AN ANIMAL!

Say it!

Finding good in (almost) everything and everyone

When it rains, look for rainbows.
When it is dark, look for stars.

I have no problem finding words, but I spent the first half of my life in silence worrying about saying the wrong ones. Now, I say 99% of what's in my heart and my head and I am glad I do it.

We need to say what is on our minds, especially the good stuff. So, say it. Every day you should tell someone in your life how much you appreciate them and their uniqueness.

Tell them you love them.
Tell them you're sorry.
Tell them they are amazing.
Tell them you miss them.

Be grateful for your life and the blessings you have and be a blessing to others.

If you believe, thank God.
Say it! Touch someone's heart with words.

> "The most beautiful things in the world cannot be seen or touched, they are felt with the heart!"
>
> —Antoine de Saint-Exupery, *The Little Prince*

Failure – A Blessing

"What if I fall? Oh, but my darling, what if you fly?"

—Erin Hanson

You do not grow in a bubble. Safe spaces are only a rest stop for you to catch your breath, dust yourself off, and then get back out there with the rest of us and push those limits even if it means stinkin' it up once in a while. Set limits but then push them hard. If you haven't done something that scared you or made you uncomfortable lately, then you will never reach your full potential.

"If you are afraid to fail you will never do the things you are capable of doing."

—John Wooden

That fear holding you back must be eliminated. You might worry that if people knew your thoughts or things you have done in the past, they would reject you. Screw them! We all have a past, and we've all made mistakes. We are not perfect. Those who judge and reject you are making yet another mistake to add to their own pile of stupidity and regret.

What's important is the journey you are on right now, not where you have been or where you are going. What's also important is that you enjoy the journey.

> **"Every saint has a past, every sinner has a future."**
>
> —Oscar Wilde

Know this: You have not failed until you quit. You will fall, and you will get up again. You may repeat this many times and you may not want to try again because some people will laugh at you. Those who laugh at other people's failures are usually those who are miserable in their conformity and too cowardly to go for their dreams so they sure as hell don't want you going for yours. Keep getting back up and trying.

You may hear laughter as you get up time after time to try again, but eventually the only laughter you hear will be your own as you finally take flight and soar to great heights. Yes, my darlings, you will fly.

I am a nice girl. I carry an axe.

www.ingramcontent.com/pod-product-compliance
Lightning Source LLC
LaVergne TN
LVHW041536060526
838200LV00037B/1013